Diet recommendations for TCM - Heart - Blood deficiency

Please check these recommendations always with a TCM nutrition consultant, therapist, doctor or dietician. The recipes and the list of ingredients are supporting also the conventional medical therapy. The calorie disclosures of fresh ingredients (fruit and vegetables) vary according to quality and time of harvest. The contents were checked by a dietician and a nutrition consultant for the Traditional Chinese Medicine (TCM).

Author:
©2017 Josef Miligui
www.ebns.at

AF285336

Source:
The lists are created from the EBNS database for nutritional counseling. The database is used by dietitians, therapists and doctors for advising the patient / client.

Literature:
The specialist literature and the training documents of the German and Austrian dietary and traditional Chinese medicine serve as a knowledge base. We have used the documents as a basis of knowledge, adapted it to our experience and completed them.
http://di-book.com

Title Photo:
©2008 Erika Weixlbaumer

Production and publishing:
BoD – Books on Demand, Norderstedt
ISBN: 9783752811155

Diet recommendations for TCM - Heart - Blood deficiency

1 Treatment strategy

Strengthen the blood and heart (see also Liver blood build-up), calm the mind, strengthen the center (spleen qi structure). Hot NO, warm LITTLE (sweet YES), cold NO (salty LITTLE), neutral u refreshing (sour LITTLE).

2 Avoid

Bitter-drying, coffee, red wine, black and green tea, lamb, cigarettes, spicy hot and hot spices, yogurt tea, alc, very salty, cheese, tropical fruits, too much sweet, oats, wheat flour (looks hot !!!), stress, screens to sleep late.

3 Breakfast   kkal. per serving

Apple sauce with raisins	73
Barley soup	265
Carrot and rice gruel soup	101
Celery juice	33
Champignon rice	410
Cous-Cous with date, coco and almondpuree	483
Reissue soup with duck	160
Reissue soup with fresh fruits	143
Reissue soup with seaweed	130
Rice congee with dried fruit	210
Rice dulse soup	190
Rice noodle soup with shiitake mushrooms	65
Rice with parsnips	206
Roasted nuts	973
Soup with egg yolk	173
Tea from ginseng	0
Tea from juniper berry	10

4 Snack

5 Lunch

6 Afternoon

7 Dinner

8 Any time

9 Recipes

(recommendable) = You can use more.
(little) = You should use less than specified or omit.

9.1 8 treasures of rice

Strengthens kidney and bladder, builds up Qi, strengthens the spleen, repels moisture, reduces internal heat, prevents cancer, builds heart, calms nerves.
Cooking time approx. 1 hour
4 portions

Quantity of ingredients
Lily bulbs 1 table spoon / 5g. ().. *
Longane 1 table spoon / 5g. (recommended)................................... *
King Solomon's-seal 1 table spoon / 5g. (yes) .... *
Yam root, yam root tuber 1 table spoon / 5g. (yes)........................... *
Coix (seeds) YiYi Ren 1 table spoon / 5g. (yes).............................. *
Rice wild (nature rice) 1 1/2 cups / 240g. (recommended).......... metal
Water 8-10 cups / 800g. (yes) .... earth

Cooking instructions:
Each one 1 tbsp: Bai He, Longan, Yu Zhu, Da Zao, Shan Yao, Lian Mi, Yi Yi Ren, Qian Shi
Add hot water and soak for about 30 minutes. Then add 1 - 2 cups of rice (normal) and simmer for 1/2 to 1 hour until the rice is very soft. Or: Cook for about 3 hours with the herbs a congee. Then the herbs do not have to be soaked.

9.2 Apple sauce with raisins

Nourishes fluids, reduces stomach heat, strengthens spleen, harmonizes stomach, moisturizes, relaxes, builds up Qi.
Cooking time approx. 25 min
Calories p. portion: 74
10 portions
Allergens: O

Quantity of ingredients
Apple (sweet) 2,2 lbs / 1000g. (yes).. earth
Water 1/2 cup / 100g. (yes) .... earth
Raisins 1/8 lbs - 2oz / 50g. (yes)... earth

Cooking instructions:
Wash, peel and quarter the apples and remove the core. Put the apples with the water in a pot. Wash the raisins with hot water and add them. Cook at low heat for about 10 minutes, then allow to cool. For children up to 10 months, mash in the blender finely. For the larger ones, crush with the potato steamer. Fill and seal in a freezer or empty yoghurt jug. Close the yoghurt jug. Freeze in the shock freezer.
If necessary, thaw at room temperature for about 6 hours. (Lasting about 4 months).
The fruit mousse is intended as dessert or intermediate meal. It has an anti-digestive effect. In case of diarrhea give better banana.

9.3   Barley soup

Works neutral to slightly warming and relaxes the Qi flow. Helps with loss of appetite and diarrhea due to spleen weakness. With weak spleen qi, one should often eat salty soups for breakfast.
Cooking time approx. 25 min
Calories p. portion: 265
2 portions
Allergens: A

Quantity of ingredients
Barley 1 cup / 120g. (recommended)... earth
Salt 1 pinch / 1g. (little)...water
Ginger fresh 1/2 teaspoon / 1g. (little)..metal
Olive oil 1 table spoon / 10g. (yes).. earth
Parsley 2 table spoons / 30g. (recommended)...........................wood
Water 1 1/2 cups / 240g. (yes)... earth

Cooking instructions:
Roast the barley in the pan, then grind it to the ground, and boil with water, some salt and ginger to a mash. Before serving add oil and parsley.

Variant: You can add a better taste to the dish if you cook it with prepared vegetable or meat broth.

9.4   Basic recipe for a chicken broth worming

Strengthens Qi and blood, is very warm.
Cooking time approx. 2-3 hours
Calories p. portion: 90
9 portions
Allergens: L

Quantity of ingredients
Chicken meat 1/2 piece / 600g. (recommended)........................wood
Carrot 2 pieces / 150g. (recommended).................................... earth
Leek 1 stick / 45g. (little)..metal
Celery root 1 piece / 500g. (recommended)............................... earth
Ginger fresh 2 slices / 2g. (little) ....metal
Fenugreek (Trigonella foenum-graecum) 1 teaspoon / 2g. (yes)......*
Juniper berry 1 teaspoon / 3g. (recommended)............................ fire
Bay leaf 3 pieces / 2g. (yes) ....*
Water 4 cup / 900g. (yes)... earth

Cooking instructions:
Remove chicken parts from fat. Place chicken pieces in a saucepan
with hot water and heat till it boils briefly, skimming any resulting foam.
Add coarsely chopped vegetables and all spices and cook over medium
heat for 2 to 3 hours. Strain the finished soup. Throw away vegetables
and bones.
Tip: If you want to use the meat as a soup insert, take out after 45
minutes and return only the bones in the soup.
Refrigerate for later use.

9.5   Basic recipe for a duck broth

Forces Qi, strengthens blood and fluids, nourishes Yin, forces stomach,
cools heat, strengthens spleen and liver.
Cooking time approx. 2-3 hours
Calories p. portion: 61
6 portions
Allergens: L

Quantity of ingredients
Water 2 cup / 450g. (yes).. earth
Duck (heart) 5/8 oz / 200g. (recommended).............................wood
Duck (slaughtered) 1/4 lbs - 4oz / 100g. (recommended)...........wood
Carrot 2 pieces / 100g. (recommended).................................... earth
Celery root 1/2 piece / 600g. (recommended)............................ earth

Cooking instructions:
Cook duck pieces with vegetables for 2-3 hours. Sift broth through a fine sieve and refrigerate for later use.

The innards can be reused: You cut them finely and leaves them for a few minutes with fresh vegetables in the broth draw. Sprinkle with parsley before serving.

9.6 Basic recipe for a reissue soup (Congee)

Warms the stomach and spleen, harmonizes the intestine, forces Qi, reduces moisture.
Cooking time approx. 2-4 hours
Calories p. portion: 140
3 portions

Quantity of ingredients
Rice variety any 1 cup / 120g. (recommended)..........................metal
Water 6 cups / 700g. (yes) .... earth

Cooking instructions:
Cook rice and water in a ratio of about 1: 6. The amount of water determines the thickness of the mash (matter of taste).
Put the rice in a saucepan with a heavy lid. It is important to simmer the rice after a short boil on the slightest flame, otherwise it burns.
Boil the rice for 2-4 hours. The longer he cooks, the more he strengthens.
If you want to eat the dish for breakfast, you can put the rice on just before bedtime.
To be on the safe side, you should first check the behavior of your pot and cooker under observation for a similar amount of time, so that nothing burns.
Refrigerate for later use.

9.7 Beef soup with carrots, leeks, bay leaves

Strengthens spleen Qi, strengthens blood and Qi, moisturizes, relaxes, builds up Qi, spreads, strengthens spleen and liver, regulates Qi flow, strengthens stomach Qi.
Cooking time approx. 2-3 hours
Calories p. portion: 194
5 portions

Quantity of ingredients

Beef meat 1 lbs / 500g. (little)... earth
Carrot 2 pieces / 200g. (recommended).................................... earth
Leek 1/2 piece / 150g. (little) ....metal
Bay leaf 3 leaves / 1g. (yes) ....*
Corn Grease (Polenta) 1 table spoon / 10g. (yes)...................... earth
Water 2 cup / 450g. (yes).. earth
Salt 1 pinch / 0,5g. (little)..water

Cooking instructions:
In a saucepan with water (enough to cover the meat), add beef soup meat or leg slice and simmer for a moment; then pour off the broth, rinse the meat with hot water (this will save you from foaming), clean the pot and put the meat in hot water again; add chopped carrot, leek, corn and bay leaf; simmer until the meat is cooked.

9.8   Black-eyed beans stew

Strengthens spleen and kidney, is very nutritious, warms the stomach and spleen, harmonizes the intestine, forces Qi, strengthens stomach and kidney, strengthens spleen and kidney.
Cooking time approx. 20 min
Calories p. portion: 140
5 portions

Quantity of ingredients

Black-eyed peas 1 cup / 100g. (yes)...water
Rice variety any 1 1/2 cups / 200g. (recommended) ....metal
Water 10 cups / 1000g. (yes)... earth

Cooking instructions:
Soak the beans overnight and strain.

In a ratio of 1: 2, simmer the beans together with the rice in the Water. Depending on how hot the flame is and how thin the dish should be, more water must be added.

Variation: Add vegetables fried in oil, such as carrots, celery tubers, onions or leeks.

9.9   Boiled fillet (Austrian classic Tafelspitz)

Strengthens spleen Qi, strengthens blood and Qi, moisturizes, relaxes, builds up Qi, spreads, forces Qi, forces spleen, relieves inflammation, moisturizes.
Cooking time approx. 3 hours
Calories p. portion: 454
8 portions
Allergens: L

Quantity of ingredients
Onion white 1 piece / 50g. (yes) ....metal
Corn germ oil 1 table spoon / 10g. (yes)..................................... earth
Water 32 cup - 1 gallon / 0g. (yes)... earth
Beef meat 5,4 lbs - 70oz cap of rump / 1800g. (little) .... earth
Beef meatbones 4n slices with bone marrow / 0g. (little)............ earth
Salt 1 pinch / 0,5g. (little)..water
Peppercorns 15 pieces / 0g. (yes) ....metal
Parsnip 1 piece / 0g. (recommended).. fire
Carrot 2 pieces / 0g. (recommended) .... earth
Celery root 1 slice / 0g. (recommended) .... earth
Parsley root 2 pieces / 0g. (yes) .... earth
Leek 1/2 stick / 0g. (little)..metal
Chives 1 table spoon (chopped) / 7g. (yes)...............................metal
Potato 2,2 lbs / 1000g. (yes)...earth
Sunflower oil 2 table spoons / 20g. (yes) .... earth
Salt 1 pinch / 0,5g. (little)...water

Cooking instructions:
Halve the onions, but do not peel. Brown onions in a pan with fat on the cut surfaces very dark. Wash meat and bones briefly with warm water, drain.
Heat the water till it boils, put in meat and cook gently. Always scoop up rising foam. As soon as no more foam rises, add peppercorns and the onion. Clean and cut root and leeks and add after about two and a half hours cooking time. Simmer for another half hour.
Remove boiled beef from the soup, pour through a sieve and season with salt. Cut roots into bite-sized pieces. Add the soup together with the marrow bones and leave it under the boiling point. Cut the boiled beef into finger-
thick slices against the grain, place in the soup, heat again, sprinkle with a little chives.In addition, cook and peel the potatoes in salted water. Stomp roughly or cut finely. Fry in a pan with the oil crispy.

9.10 Carp soup

Nourishing and slightly warming, strengthens the middle and the lower heater, removes moisture.
Cooking time approx. 2 hours
Calories p. portion: 499
2 portions
Allergens: DO

Quantity of ingredients
Carp 1,1 lbs / 500g. (recommended) ....water
Salt 1 pinch / 1g. (little)..water
Vinegar (Apple vinegar) 1 teaspoon / 3g. (little) ....wood
Thyme 1 Twig / 3g. (yes)..*
Juniper berry 8 pieces / 3g. (recommended)............................... fire
Carrot 2 pieces / 200g. (recommended).................................... earth
Leek 1 piece / 200g. (little) ....metal
Onion white 1 piece / 60g. (yes) ....metal
Ginger fresh 1/2 teaspoon / 2g. (little)................................metal
Bay leaf 3 leaves / 1g. (yes) ....*
White wine 1/2 cup / 125g. (little).....................................wood
Basil 3 leaves / 1g. (yes) ....metal

Cooking instructions:
Preparation: When shopping at the fishmonger, remove the fillets from a medium-sized, whole carp and also pack the fish head, spine with bones and tail.

Cut the fillets into 1 cm cubes; salt and set aside.

Place fish head, backbone and tail of carp in plenty of cold water; heat till it boils and scoop the foam; add a dash of vinegar, a fresh sprig of thyme, juniper berries; Add carrot, a piece of leek and chopped onion; add a thick slice of ginger, some peppercorns, 1 bay leaf, salt; simmer for about 1 1/2 hours and pour the stock through a sieve.

Put the carp pieces in a saucepan; pour a shot of white wine; Add rose paprika, basil leaves, finely ground carrots, dried thyme and the stock and warm; Boil the ingredients for about 5 minutes until the fish pieces are cooked.
Variants: Thicken the soup with kudzu or mashed potatoes.
This fits: baguette and dry white wine.

9.11 Carrot and rice gruel soup

Warms the stomach and spleen, harmonizes the intestine, forces Qi, reduces moisture, strengthens spleen and liver, regulates Qi flow, moisturizes, relaxes, builds up Qi, spreads.
Cooking time approx. 10 min
Calories p. portion: 101
1 portions

Quantity of ingredients
Basic recipe for a rice soup (Congee) 1 cup / 120g. (yes)................*
Carrot 2 pieces / 100g. (recommended).................................... earth
Salt 1 teaspoon / 4g. (little)...water

Cooking instructions:
Peel and grate carrots. Heat the rice soup (according to the basic recipe) till it boils and add the grated carrots and salt. Cook for 10 minutes.

9.12 Carrot rice with chicken

Strengthens spleen and liver, regulates Qi flow, moisturizes, relaxes, spreads, forces Qi, blood and Jing, medium heater, builds up spleen and stomach, forces Qi, reduces moisture, cools heat, nourishes fluids.
Cooking time approx. 30 min
Calories p. portion: 116
2 portions
Allergens: G

Quantity of ingredients
Carrot (Early Carrot) 3/8 lbs - 6oz / 150g. (recommended)......... earth
Chicken meat 1/8 lbs - 2oz / 40g. (recommended)..................... wood
Butter organic 2 teaspoons / 6g. (yes) .... earth
Water 1 cup / 250g. (yes)... earth
Rice round grain 1 oz / 30g. (recommended)..............................metal
Orange juice 2 table spoons / 20g. (little)................................... wood

Cooking instructions:
Clean, wash and peel the carrots and grate. Cut the chicken breast into small cubes, sauté in 1 teaspoon of butter, add the carrots and rice. Add the water and heat till it boils. Cook over low heat for about 20 minutes. Put the carrot rice on a dish, add the remaining butter and orange juice.

9.13 Celery juice

Strengthens stomach Qi, moisturizes, relaxes, builds up Qi, spreads.
Cooking time approx. 5 min
Calories p. portion: 33
1 portions
Allergens: L

Quantity of ingredients
Celery root 1/2 piece / 200g. (recommended) .... earth
Water 1 cup / 120g. (yes) .... earth
Salt 1 pinch / 0,5g. (little) ....water

Cooking instructions:
Peel celeriac and cut into pieces and juice. Mix with water and salt as needed.

9.14 Champignon rice

Strengthens spleen, builds up Qi, directs heat down, strengthens stomach Qi, cools blood heat.
Cooking time approx. 30 min
Calories p. portion: 410
2 portions
Allergens: L

Quantity of ingredients
Onion white 1 piece / 50g. (yes) ....metal
Bay leaf 2 pieces / 1g. (yes) ....*
Clove 2 pieces / 1g. (little) ....metal
Basic recipe for a vegetable soup (nutritious) 7/8 lbs / 350g. (yes)....*
Rice (whole grain) 5/8 oz / 200g. (recommended).....................metal
Champignon 1/8 lbs - 2oz / 60g. (yes) .... earth
Parsley 1/2 oz / 20g. (recommended) .... wood
Pepper (ground) 1 pinch / 0,2g. (yes) ....metal

Cooking instructions:
Plug in the cloves in the onion. Heat the vegetable stock with the onion and the bay leaves till it boils. Add the rice to the boiling liquid, reduce the temperature to the lowest level and stir with the lid closed for 20-25 minutes. In the meantime, wash the mushrooms, clean them, slice them, sauté briefly with a little water or sauté. Wash the parsley and chop finely. Remove the onion from the rice, add the mushrooms and the parsley, season with pepper.

9.15 Chicken soup with angelica root and buckthorn fruit

Strengthens spleen and nourishes the blood and Yin of the liver, forces Qi and blood, is very warming.
Cooking time approx. 1 1/2 hours
Calories p. portion: 77
3 portions
Allergens: LO

Quantity of ingredients
Basic recipe for a chicken soup (warming) 2 cup / 500g. (yes)..........*
Angelica root 1/8 oz / 5g. (yes)...*
Bocksdorn fruits (Fructus Lycii) 1/8 lbs - 2oz / 50g. ....wood

Cooking instructions:
When you cook chicken broth according to basic recipes add angelica root and willowberry fruits in the last 40 minutes.

Ingestion: Drink 2-3 cups of broth daily.

9.16 Chicken soup with egg yolk and parsley

Forces Qi and blood, is very warming, nourishes blood and liver, harmonizes liver and spleen, forces eyesight, preserves the fluids, contracts.
Cooking time approx. 10 min
Calories p. portion: 118
2 portions
Allergens: CL

Quantity of ingredients
Basic recipe for a chicken soup (warming) 2 cup / 500g. (yes)..........*
Chicken yolk 1 piece / 10g. (yes)... earth
Parsley 1 table spoon / 10g. (recommended)............................wood

Cooking instructions:
Cook the chicken broth according to the basic recipe.
Heat broth and bubble the egg yolk. Sprinkle the chopped parsley over it and let it rest for about 2 minutes. Drink in small sips.

9.17 Chicken soup with green spelt, parsley and sake

Forces Qi and blood, is very warming, nourishes liver-blood, preserves the fluids, contracts, scatters and move Qi, moisturizes, reduces cold-evil, softens knots.
Cooking time approx. 1 1/2 hours
Calories p. portion: 150
2 portions
Allergens: AL

Quantity of ingredients
Basic recipe for a chicken soup (warming) 2 cup / 500g. (yes)..........*
Green spelt 4 table spoons / 30g. (little)....................................wood
Parsley 2 table spoons / 14g. (recommended)...........................wood
Sake 1 dash / 2g. (yes) ....metal

Cooking instructions:
Cook the chicken broth according to the basic recipe. Add the ingredients in the soup and simmer 10 min.

9.18 Clear oxen tail soup with buckthorn fruit

Forces Qi, nourishes the liver blood, good for ocular fibrillation or dry eyes, muscle tension or calf cramps due to blood deficiency.
Cooking time approx. 1-2 hours
Calories p. portion: 217
6 portions
Allergens: O

Quantity of ingredients
Basic recipe for a beef soup (warming) 4 cup / 1000g. (little) ....*
Beef Oxtail pieces 1,1 lbs / 500g. (little)....................................earth
Shiitake, dried 4-5 pieces / 4g. (yes)..earth
Onion white 1 piece / 60g. (yes) ....metal
Sake 2 table spoons / 20g. (yes) ....metal
Ginger fresh 1/2 teaspoon / 2g. (little)..metal
Bocksdorn fruits (Fructus Lycii, Goji, goji berry dried 1 table spoon / 8g. wood

Cooking instructions:
Soak shiitake mushrooms. Blanch oxtail slices (This removes fat and impurities). Cook in the beef broth for 1-2 hours.
Then add the spring onions, shiitake mushrooms, rice wine, buckthorn fruits and ginger and simmer gently.

9.19 Cous-Cous with date, coco and almondpuree

Forces Yin.
Cooking time approx. 10 min
Calories p. portion: 484
3 portions
Allergens: AHO

Quantity of ingredients
Couscous 1 1/2 cups / 240g. (yes) ....wood
Water 4 cups / 400g. (yes) .... earth
Dates dried 6 pieces / 20g. (yes)... earth
Coconut flakes 2 table spoons / 30g. (yes) .... earth
Almond puree 2 table spoons / 20g. (yes)................................. earth
Olive oil 2 teaspoons / 20g. (yes)... earth
Apple (sweet) 1 piece grated / 120g. (yes)................................ earth
Vanilla 1 knife tip / 0,2g. (yes)..*

Cooking instructions:
Put couscous and olive oil in a large bowl and pour boiling water over
them. Let it swell for 10 minutes. Crush dates and grate apple. Loosen
up cous-cous with a fork. Mix in dates, coconut flakes, apple and
almond paste.
Sweet to taste. Spices and flavors: vanilla, little chili

Winter variation: pear,
Summer variation: apricot, nectarine

9.20 Indian Dal soup

Reduces internal heat and moisture, softens, passes downwardly,
strengthens spleen and liver, regulates Qi flow, moisturizes, relaxes,
builds up Qi, spreads, forces liver and kidney, reduces damp heat.
Cooking time approx. 30 min
Calories p. portion: 256
2 portions
Allergens: EN

Quantity of ingredients
Lentils 3/8 lbs - 6oz / 175g. (yes)..water
Sesame oil 2 table spoons / 30g. (yes)...................................... earth
Carrot 1 piece / 100g. (recommended) .... earth
Onion (shallot) 1 piece / 15g. (yes)..metal
Water 1 1/2 cups / 200g. (yes)... earth

Ginger fresh 2 slices / 1g. (little) ....metal
Salt 1 pinch / 0,5g. (little)...water
Soy sauce 1 teaspoon / 3g. (little)...water
Parsley 1 teaspoon (chopped) / 3g. (recommended)................wood
Thyme 1 teaspoon / 3g. (yes)..*
Basil 1 table spoon / 5g. (yes) ....metal

Cooking instructions:
Soak the lentils overnight.
in a hot pot, carrot, onion and a little ginger fry, pour water. Add the lentils and cook until soft. Add salt or soy sauce and cook for another 10 minutes.
Stir in parsley before serving; Sprinkle thyme or basil over it.
Variant: Other herbs such as sage, rosemary or lovage allow a variety of flavors.

9.21 Japanese algae soup

Strengthens spleen and liver, regulates Qi flow, moisturizes, relaxes, builds up Qi, spreads, nourishes the lungs and spleen, distributes mucus, dissolves mucus, dissolves stagnation, directs upwards, gets Qi moving und Yang.
Cooking time approx. 20 min
Calories p. portion: 47
3 portions

Quantity of ingredients
Wakame 1 oz / 25g. (yes)...water
Water 2 cup / 450g. (yes).. earth
Onion (shallot) 1-2 pcs. / 30g. (yes).............................metal
Radish (white, green, purple-red) 1/8 lbs - 2oz / 50g. (yes)........metal
Carrot 2 pieces / 180g. (recommended).................................... earth
Miso 2 table spoons / 20g. (yes)...............................water
Parsley 2 table spoons / 20g. (recommended)..........................wood
Onion (spring onion) 1 table spoon (sliced)..............................metal

Cooking instructions:
Soak wakame in water for a few minutes, remove and bring the water to the boil. Add finely chopped onions and wakame, radishes and carrots, cut into thin strips, and simmer for another 10 minutes. Dissolve miso in a little cooled cooking water and add it at the end. Sprinkle with parsley and spring onions.

9.22 Kudzu soup in the morning

Moisturizes, relaxes, builds up Qi, spreads, forces stomach, harmonizes middle, reduces internal heat, detoxifies, softens, passes downwardly.
Cooking time approx. 5 min
Calories p. portion: 12
1 portions
Allergens: E

Quantity of ingredients
Water 1 cup / 250g. (yes) .... earth
Soy sauce 1 dash / 2g. (little) ....water
Umeboshi paste 1 knife tip / 2g. (little) ....water

Cooking instructions:
Mix kudzu with cold water and heat till it boils while stirring. Once it is glassy, remove from heat and let cool. Season with Tamari and Umeboshipaste or crushed umeboshi plums

There is always the possibility to support your stomach and intestines with this recipe, taken before the right breakfast.
A morning cure for stomach and mucous membranes. Fix the base balance.

9.23 Lentils and rice stew

Strengthens spleen and liver, regulates Qi flow, moisturizes, relaxes, builds up Qi, spreads, warms the stomach and spleen, harmonizes the intestine, forces Qi, reduces moisture, brings the liver Qi in motion, cools heat.
Cooking time approx. 25 min
Calories p. portion: 232
3 portions
Allergens: LNO

Quantity of ingredients
Lentils 1/4 lbs - 4oz / 100g. (yes) ....water
Water 5 cups / 500g. (yes) .... earth
Rice variety any 1 cup / 120g. (recommended) ....metal
Sesame oil 1 table spoon / 10g. (yes) .... earth
Carrot 2 pieces / 150g. (recommended) .... earth
Celery sticks 2 rods / 20g. (yes) .... earth

Cumin (Caraway seed) 1 pinch / 0,2g. (yes)..............................metal
Salt 1 pinch / 0,5g. (little)..water
Vinegar (Apple vinegar) 1 dash / 2g. (little)...............................wood
Parsley 2 table spoons / 18g. (recommended)..........................wood

Cooking instructions:
Soak the dry lentils the day before.
Heat sesame oil in a hot pot; cut carrot and celery into small pieces and
sauté; add rice, a pinch of cumin and lentils and heat till it boils.
If the lenses are soft, add salt; season with a little vinegar and garnish
with parsley.

Variant: In summer you can omit the cumin and add fresh green peas,
Chinese cabbage or celery.

9.24 Mung bean stew

Dissipates excess heat, is very nutritious, reduces heat and poison,
softens, passes downwardly, warms the stomach and spleen,
harmonizes the intestine, forces Qi, reduces moisture.
Cooking time approx. 2 hours
Calories p. portion: 665
2 portions

Quantity of ingredients
Mung bean 5/8 lbs - 8oz - 500g / 300g. (yes)...........................water
Sunflower oil 2 table spoons / 30g. (yes)...................................earth
Amaranth 1/2 teaspoon / 2g. (recommended)..............................fire
Fennel seeds ground 1/2 teaspoon / 2g. (little)..........................earth
Cumin (Caraway seed) 1/2 teaspoon / 2g. (yes).......................metal
Coriander 1/2 teaspoon / 2g. (yes)..metal
Rice round grain 1/2 cup / 60g. (recommended).......................metal
Water 3 cups / 300g. (yes)...earth
Ginger fresh 1 inch / 3g. (little)..metal
Kombu seaweed (Saccharina japonica) 1 inch / 2g. (yes)..........water
Salt 1 pinch / 0,5g. (little)..water
Parsley 1 table spoon / 3g. (recommended).............................wood

Cooking instructions:
Soak mung beans overnight.
Heat sunflower oil in a hot pot. Stir in the amaranth, fennel seeds,
cumin and coriander and fry briefly.
admit basmati rice, some ginger and mung beans and roast briefly.

Pour water and heat till it boils.
Add a piece of kombu alga and salt.
Simmer for 1-1/2 hours.
Garnish with parsley or coriander.

9.25 Pumpkin slices with spicy rice

Forces lungs and spleen, diuretic, forces Qi, protects liver, warms the stomach and spleen, harmonizes the intestine, forces Qi, reduces moisture, directs upwards.
Cooking time approx. 45 min
Calories p. portion: 438
4 portions
Allergens: AG

Quantity of ingredients
Clarified butter 1/2 teaspoon / 5g. (little) .... earth
Saffron 1 Sachet / 0,1g. (yes).. earth
Turmeric (yellow root) 1 teaspoon / 2g. (little) .... *
Rice Basmati 1 cup / 120g. (recommended) .... metal
Water 1 cup / 120g. (yes).. earth
Salt 1/2 teaspoon / 2g. (little)..water
Pumpkin 6-8 slices / 400g. (yes)... earth
Barley flour 1 cup / 10g. (yes).. earth
Breadcrumbs (wheat bread, bread roll) 1 cup / 10g. (yes).......... wood
Salt 1/2 teaspoon / 2g. (little)..water
Pepper (ground) 1 pinch / 1g. (yes) .... metal
Butter organic 1 table spoon / 10g. (yes) .... earth
Cream, sweet 30% 1 1/2 cup / 300g. (little)...................................... *
Barley flour 2 table spoons / 20g. (yes)..................................... earth
Chives 2 table spoons / 20g. (yes).. metal
Dill 2 table spoons / 20g. (little).. metal

Cooking instructions:
Melt the fat in a small saucepan, add saffron and turmeric, lightly roast over medium heat for about 1-2 minutes to allow the aromas to develop (note: the spices should never be burnt). Add the rice for about 2 minutes stir fry, add the salt, stir briefly and add the water, stir and close the pot with a lid. Cook at low to medium heat until the water is almost completely absorbed, then remove from the heat and set aside with the lid still closed and let it swell. Do not stir! When the water is completely absorbed, the rice is ready!

Mix flour, bread crumbs, salt and pepper. Moisten the pumpkin slices with water or mashed egg, turn the slices in the flour mixture and fry gently in butter until golden brown and the pumpkin is soft. Melt the butter in a small saucepan, brown the barley flour in it and remove from heat, add the sour cream, season with salt, pepper, add the chopped herbs and pour the sauce over the fried pumpkin slices. Serve with the rice.

9.26 Pumpkin soup

Forces lungs and spleen, diuretic, forces Qi, protects liver, forces Qi, forces spleen, relieves inflammation, moisturizes, relaxes, builds up Qi, spreads, strengthens spleen and liver, regulates Qi flow, moisturizes, relaxes, builds up Qi, spreads.
Cooking time approx. 1 hour
Calories p. portion: 105
3 portions

Quantity of ingredients
Pumpkin 3/4 lbs / 300g. (yes) .... earth
Carrot 2 pieces / 100g. (recommended) .... earth
Potato 2 pieces / 120g. (yes) .... earth
Olive oil 1 table spoon / 10g. (yes) .... earth
Onion white 1 piece / 50g. (yes) ....metal
Water 1 cup / 120g. (yes) .... earth
Parsley 1 table spoon / 7g. (recommended) .... wood
Anise (Common Fennel) 1 pinch / 1g. (little) .... earth
Salt 1 pinch / 1g. (little) ....water

Cooking instructions:
Add the olive oil to the pan, add the diced pumpkin, diced carrots and potatoes. Roast them shortly, add the finely chopped onion, fill with water, add enough water to cover the vegetables at least 3 finger-widths. Boil at low heat.

Season with sea salt, add small cutted parsley, a pinch of anise (little). Allow to simmer for about 35 minutes. Then purée the soup and add some water, depending on the consistency of the soup.

9.27 Red grape juice with egg yolk

Tonifies Yin and Qi, brings blood into motion, exudes moisture, detoxifying, hematinic.
Cooking time approx. 5 min
Calories p. portion: 271
1 portions
Allergens: C

Quantity of ingredients
Grape juice red 1 cup / 250g. (recommended)........................... earth
Chicken yolk 1 piece / 25g. (yes)... earth

Cooking instructions:
Whisk egg yolks in grape juice.

9.28 Reissue soup with duck

Nourishes Yin, warms the stomach and spleen, harmonizes the intestine, forces Qi, reduces moisture, nourishes blood and liver, harmonizes liver and spleen, moisturizes, relaxes, builds up Qi, spreads.
Cooking time approx. 1 1/2 hours
Calories p. portion: 161
6 portions
Allergens: EG

Quantity of ingredients
Rice round grain 1 cup / 100g. (recommended) ....metal
Water 8 cups / 900g. (yes) .... earth
Duck (slaughtered) 5/8 lbs - 8oz / 250g. (recommended)...........wood
Shiitake, dried 4-6 pieces / 5g. (yes).. earth
Parsley 2 table spoons / 12g. (recommended)...........................wood
Butter organic 1 teaspoon / 3g. (yes)... earth
Soy sauce 1 dash / 2g. (little) ....water

Cooking instructions:
Soak shiitake mushrooms. Prepare rice soup according to the basic recipe. Add duck meat and shiitake mushrooms for the last 30 minutes. Add oyster mushrooms, parsley and a little butter at the very end. Season with soy sauce.
Variant: Add soaked and cooked adzuki beans. They enhance the diuretic effect.

9.29 Reissue soup with fresh fruits

Forces kidney and bladder, strengthens Qi and kidney Jing,
moisturizes, relaxes, builds up Qi, reduces internal heat, produces
humors, moisturizes, spreads, expels cold, dissolves stagnation, drives
sweat, stimulates nerves.
Cooking time approx. 1 1/2 hours
Calories p. portion: 143
4 portions
Allergens: G

Quantity of ingredients
Rice wild (nature rice) 1 cup / 100g. (recommended)..................metal
Water 8 cups / 900g. (yes) .... earth
Apple (sweet) 1 1/2 cups / 200g. (yes)...................................... earth
Butter organic 1 table spoon / 10g. (yes) .... earth
Vanilla 1 pinch / 0,2g. (yes) ....*
Sugar cane sugar 2 teaspoons / 6g. (recommended)............... earth

Cooking instructions:
Prepare rice congee according to basic recipe.

At the end, add finely chopped fruits to the season, vanilla, chili and
butter; sweet to taste.

Variant: With nuts, the dish can always be made richer and more filling.

Effect: Cooked or steamed fruits are easier to digest and act better
than raw. For some fruits, which are particularly suitable for hot summer
days - such as melons and berries - it is still advisable to add the fruits
only to a hot porridge.
Other types of fruit - such as apples, pears, plums and cherries - can
also be simmered for a while.

9.30 Reissue soup with seaweed

Forces Qi and blood, reduces cold, forces spleen, liver and stomach,
strengthens blood and Qi, regulates Qi, warms spleen and kidney,
dissolves stagnation, directs upwards.
Cooking time approx. 4-5 hours
Calories p. portion: 130
6 portions
Allergens: L

Quantity of ingredients

Beef meatbones 3/4 lbs / 10g. (little).. earth
Beef soup meat 7/8 lbs / 400g. (little)..................................... earth
Parsley 1/4 Bunch / 25g. (recommended)............................... wood
Juniper berry 4 / 2g. (recommended).. fire
Carrot 2 pieces / 180g. (recommended)................................... earth
Celery root 1/4 lbs / 100g. (recommended).............................. earth
Onion (spring onion) 1/2 piece / 10g. (yes) ....metal
Peppercorns 4 / 1g. (yes)..metal
Lovage 1 Twig / 3g. (little) ....metal
Wakame 1 inch / 3g. (yes)...water
Rice variety any 2 table spoons / 20g. (recommended)............metal
Water 4 cup / 900g. (yes)... earth

Cooking instructions:
Boil parsley in water. Add the juniper berries, meat bones, a piece of
soup, carrot and a piece of celery tuber, a separately tanned onion half,
a few peppery grains, a belly and a piece of wakame algae; Allow 4-8
hours to simmer and then strain. Add the rice and simmer for another
1/2 hour.
Keep the stock in the refrigerator.
Variant: If you remove the meat after 1-2 hours, you can still dice it well
and use it later as a supporter.

9.31 Rice congee with chicken liver and buckthorn fruit

Warms the stomach and spleen, harmonizes the intestine, forces Qi,
reduces moisture, nourishes liver-blood, nourishes and forces liver,
forces kidney, forces blood, makes eyes clear.
Cooking time approx. 3 hours
Calories p. portion: 176
3 portions
Allergens: EO

Quantity of ingredients

Basic recipe for a rice soup (Congee) 5 cups / 800g. (yes) ....*
Chicken liver 1/2 cup / 60g. (yes)... earth
Bocksdorn fruits (Fructus Lycii) 1/2 cup / 60g. (recommended) .. wood
Soy sauce 1 dash / 3g. (little) ....water

Cooking instructions:
Cook basic recipe for rice congee with the chicken liver and wolfberry
fruits; Season with soy sauce.

9.32 Rice congee with dried fruit

Warms the stomach and spleen, harmonizes the intestine, forces Qi, reduces moisture, nourishes blood and Yi, harmonizes lungs Qi, strengthens Qi and kidney Jing, moisturizes, relaxes, builds up Qi, spreads.
Cooking time approx. 10 min
Calories p. portion: 210
2 portions
Allergens: GO

Quantity of ingredients
Basic recipe for a rice soup (Congee) 4 cups / 500g. (yes) .... *
Butter organic 1/2 teaspoon / 5g. (yes).................................... earth
Apricot dried 6 table spoons / 50g. (little)................................ earth
Water 1/2 cup / 50g. (yes)... earth
Maple syrup 1 dash / 3g. (yes) .... earth

Cooking instructions:
Cook rice congee according to basic recipe.

Melt a small amount of butter over a low heat and briefly fry small dried fruit with 1/2 cup of water. Add the amount of rice porridge desired for the meal and heat. Serve hot and sweeten with maple syrup if necessary.
Variant: In addition fresh fruit with braise.

9.33 Rice dulse soup

Strengthens spleen and liver, regulates Qi flow, relaxes, builds up Qi, spreads, dries out, passes downwardly, strengthens stomach Qi, warms the stomach and spleen, harmonizes the intestine, forces Qi, reduces moisture.
Cooking time approx. 5 min
Calories p. portion: 190
2 portions
Allergens: L

Quantity of ingredients
Basic recipe for a rice soup (Congee) 4 cups / 500g. (yes) .... *
Basic recipe for a vegetable soup (nutritious) 2 cup / 500g. (yes)...... *
Dulse (seaweed) 2 table spoons / 15g. (little) .... water

Cooking instructions:
Worm up a portion of pre-cooked basic recipe for a ricesoupe (congee) and a portion pre-cooked basic recipe for a vegetable soup. Bake the dulse in the oven at 220 degrees for 3 minutes. Spread the crisp dulse over the rice.

9.34 Rice noodle soup with shiitake mushrooms

Strengthens spleen and liver, regulates Qi flow, relaxes, builds up Qi, spreads, dries out, passes downwardly, strengthens stomach Qi, nourishes Yin of the lungs, stomach and colon, supports digestion, reduces internal wind.
Cooking time approx. 20 min
Calories p. portion: 66
2 portions
Allergens: L

Quantity of ingredients
Rice noodles 2 handful / 20g. (yes) ....metal
Shiitake, dried 4-6 pieces / 5g. (yes)... earth
Basic recipe for a vegetable soup (nutritious) 1 1/2 cups / 240g. (yes)*
Chinese cabbage 1 cup / 60g. (yes) .... earth
Lovage 1 teaspoon / 3g. (little) ....metal
Miso 2 table spoons / 18g. (yes)...water

Cooking instructions:
Soak rice noodles and shiitake mushrooms separately in cold water. Heat the vegetable broth and add the soaked shiitake mushrooms cut into strips and simmer gently. Cut Chinese cabbage into noodles, add lovage green and rice noodles and let it steep for a while. Before serving, stir in Miso dissolved in a little cooled water. Recommendation: Suitable at the beginning of each meal, also for breakfast

9.35 Rice soup with grated carrots and fresh herbs

Strengthens spleen and liver, regulates Qi flow, moisturizes, relaxes, builds up Qi, spreads, forces kidney and bladder.
Cooking time approx. 5 min
Calories p. portion: 131
4 portions
Allergens: EG

Quantity of ingredients
Rice wild (nature rice) 1 cup / 100g. (recommended)...............metal
Water 6 cups / 700g. (yes) .... earth
Carrot 1 piece / 100g. (recommended) .... earth
Soy sauce 1 dash / 2g. (little) ....water
Butter organic 1 teaspoon / 3g. (yes)..................................... earth
Ground 1 pinch / 0,3g. (yes)... earth
Curcuma 1 pinch / 0,2g. (recommended)...................................... *
Herbs various 1 teaspoon (chopped) / 3g. (yes)............................ *

Cooking instructions:
In a portion of rice congee according to basic recipe, softly cook a grated carrot, add butter and soy sauce.
Sprinkle with fresh herbs.

Spices and herbs: black cumin, turmeric, cardamom, parsley, sage, thyme, basil, rosemary.

Winter: parsnip, celery, onion, leek, pumpkin
Summer: tomatoes, zucchini, spring onion, radishes, arugula.

9.36 Rice with parsnips

Regulates Qi, dries out, passes downwardly, warms the stomach and spleen, harmonizes the intestine, forces Qi, reduces moisture.
moisturizes, relaxes, builds up Qi, spreads. distributes mucus, activates Wei Qi, forces Qi.
Cooking time approx. 45 min
Calories p. portion: 206
3 portions

Quantity of ingredients
Rice variety any 1 cup / 120g. (recommended)........................metal
Water 1 1/2 cups / 200g. (yes).. earth
Salt 1 pinch / 1g. (little)...water
Parsnip 3-4 pieces / 450g. (recommended) .... fire
Olive oil 1 table spoon / 10g. (yes)... earth
Sage 1 teaspoon / 3g. (yes) .... fire

Cooking instructions:
Peel the parsnips and cut into slices. Fry for a short time in oil. Add the rice and fry again for a short time. Add the water and cook it at least 30 min. Sprinkle with fresh chopped sage.

9.37 Roasted nuts

Strengthens kidney Qi, essence and brain, forces kidney, builds up essence, warms lungs, moistens the intestine, moisturizes, relaxes, builds up Qi, spreads.
Cooking time approx. 5 min
Calories p. portion: 973
2 portions
Allergens: H

Quantity of ingredients
Hazelnuts 1/4 lbs - 4oz / 100g. (yes).. earth
Cashews 1/4 lbs - 4oz / 100g. (yes)... earth
Walnuts 1/4 lbs - 4oz / 100g. (recommended)........................... earth

Cooking instructions:
Roast nuts in a pan for about 5 minutes.

9.38 Sliced chicken with walnuts and sherry

Warming and nourishing, directs the Qi upwards, forces blood, spleen and kidney.
Cooking time approx. 25 min
Calories p. portion: 304
4 portions
Allergens: EGHN

Quantity of ingredients
Butter organic 2 table spoons / 35g. (yes)................................. earth
Walnuts 2 table spoons / 25g. (recommended).......................... earth
Ginger fresh 1/2 teaspoon / 2g. (little)...metal
Onion (shallot) 2 pieces / 40g. (yes) ....metal
Salt 1 pinch / 1g. (little)...water
Chicken meat 3/4 lbs / 300g. (recommended)...........................wood
Peppers powder 1 pinch / 1g. ()...*
Sesame, white 1 teaspoon / 2g. (recommended)....................... earth
Black fungus mushroom 4 pieces / 3g. (yes)............................. earth
Shiitake, dried 4 pieces / 5g. (yes).. earth
Soy sauce 1 dash / 3g. (little) ....water
Rice (whole grain) 1 cup / 120g. (recommended)......................metal
Water 6 cups / 550g. (yes) .... earth
Salt 1 pinch / 1g. (little)...water

Cooking instructions:
Heat butter or sesame oil in a hot pan; Sauté walnuts, copious grated ginger, chopped shallots or onions; Add the salt and the sliced chicken and sauté everything; Rose paprika, roasted sesame, soaked black fungus, shiitake mushrooms or mushrooms; with a shot sherry; infuse with water; Simmer for 5 to 10 minutes until the meat is cooked; Season with soy sauce.
Place the rice in salted water, heat till it boils and let it simmer over low heat for about 15 minutes.
This fits: lamb's lettuce, Radicchio

9.39 Soup with egg yolk

Forces Qi and Yang, is very warming.
Cooking time approx. 5 min
Calories p. portion: 173
1 portions
Allergens: CO

Quantity of ingredients
Basic recipe for a beef soup (warming) 1 cup / 250g. (little) ....*
Chicken yolk 1 piece / 25g. (yes).. earth

Cooking instructions:
Warm the beef soup according to the basic recipe for a beef broth, warm it up and jell the yolk.

9.40 Spinach with Tahini

Nourishes blood and Yin, forces Zang-organs, forces stomach and intestines, harmonizes Qi, moisturizes lungs, forces Qi, forces spleen, relieves inflammation, moisturizes, relaxes, builds up Qi, spreads, nourishes blood.
Cooking time approx. 20 min
Calories p. portion: 150
4 portions
Allergens: N

Quantity of ingredients
Potato 1,1 lbs / 500g. (yes).. earth
Salt 1 pinch / 0,2g. (little)...water
Water 1 cup / 25g. (yes)... earth
Spinach 2,2 lbs / 800g. (recommended) .... earth
Sesame paste (Tahini) 2 table spoons / 20g. (recommended) ... earth

Cooking instructions:
Cook potatoes and peel. Heat water. Blanch spinach. Shake off water and let it dry and stir with sesame.

9.41 Tea from coriander

Sudorific, reduces wind.
Cooking time approx. 10 min
Calories p. portion: 2
4 portions

Quantity of ingredients
Coriander 1 teaspoon / 3g. (yes) ....metal
Water 2 cup / 500g. (yes) .... earth

Cooking instructions:
Heat the water till it boils and put it aside. Add coriander and 10 min. to let go. Sweet to taste with honey. Strain when pouring.

9.42 Tea from Fructus Lycii

Strengthens blood and fluids, regulates Qi, produces humors, calms the mind, forces Qi.
Cooking time approx. 10 min
Calories p. portion: 3
4 portions

Quantity of ingredients
Lychee 2 teaspoons / 18g. () ....*
Water 2 cup / 500g. (yes) .... earth

Cooking instructions:
Heat the water till it boils and put it aside. Add Fructus Lyecii and keep for 10 min. to let go. Sweet to taste with honey.

9.43 Tea from ginseng

Forces heart, lungs, stomach, spleen, kidney-Qi.
Cooking time approx. 20 min
Calories p. portion: 0
4 portions

Quantity of ingredients

Ginseng 2 teabags / 4g. (yes)...*

Water 2 cup / 500g. (yes).. earth

Cooking instructions:
A very mild form of taking ginseng is achieved by placing it in a thermos of hot water. You can also use the root several times, not just for a pot filling. Ideally, you should have cooked the water for 10 minutes - it is then assigned to the conversion phase of fire (TCM) - and to use non-carbonated medicinal spring water, if the quality of the water on site is not good.

Ingestion: This mild ginseng tea can be drunk throughout the day for strengthening.

9.44 Tea from ground

Reduces mucus and moist heat in the liver and gallbladder, against liver Qi stagnation, spleen qi deficiency, spleen and kidney Yang-Mangel.
Cooking time approx. 10 min
Calories p. portion: 2
4 portions

Quantity of ingredients

Ground 1 teaspoon / 3g. (yes)................................... earth

Water 2 cup / 500g. (yes).. earth

Cooking instructions:
Heat the water till it boils and put it aside. Add crushed cumin and leave for 10 min. to let go. Sweet to taste with honey. Strain when pouring.

Drink 1 cup 2 times a day.

9.45 Tea from juniper berry

Dries out, passes downwardly, activates Wei Qi.
Cooking time approx. 10 min
Calories p. portion: 10
1 portions

Quantity of ingredients

Juniper berry 1 teaspoon / 3g. (recommended)............................ fire

Water 1 cup / 125g. (yes).. earth

Cooking instructions:
A teaspoon of dried juniper berries for a cup of tea. Start cold and bring to the boil. Let it sit for 15 minutes, then strain.
This tea is unsweetened and swallowed, slowly drunk. The amount is enough for one day.

9.46 Tea from licorice (heart-strengthening)

Strengthen spleen and stomach Qi, nourishes Yin from heart and kidney, moisturizes, forces heart and kidney, reduces internal heat, preserves the fluids, contracts.
Cooking time approx. 15 min
Calories p. portion: 20
4 portions

Quantity of ingredients
Licorice root tea 2-4 teaspoons / 6g. () ....*
Dates red 2 table spoons (chopped) / 20g. (yes)........................ earth
Wheat 2 teaspoons (milled) / 16g. (recommended).................... wood
Water 2 cup / 500g. (yes) .... earth

Cooking instructions:
Simmer licorice root, red dates and wheat for 40 minutes, strain and keep the tea in the refrigerator. Throw away the ingredients.
Variant: This recipe can be supplemented with chicken broth; it will be even stronger.
Decoction: 2-4 teaspoons, sprinkle licorice with 1/2 liter of cold water, heat till it boils, cook for 1 min, leave for 10 min. Drink 1 cup twice a day.

9.47 Tea from longane

Forces spleen, builds up lung, builds up heart, calms nerves.
Cooking time approx. 10 min
Calories p. portion: 0
4 portions

Quantity of ingredients
Longane 2 teaspoons / 4g. (recommended).....................................*
Water 2 cup / 500g. (yes) .... earth

Cooking instructions:
Heat the water till it boils and put it aside. Add Longane and 10 min. to let go. Sweet to taste with honey. Strain when pouring.

9.48 Tea from rose hip

Strengthens spleen Qi.
Cooking time approx. 10 min
Calories p. portion: 2
4 portions

Quantity of ingredients
Rose hip tea 2 table spoons / 4g. (recommended).....................wood
Water 2 cup / 500g. (yes)... earth

Cooking instructions:
Heat the water till it boils and put it aside. Add rosehip and leave for 10 min. to let go. Sweet to taste with honey. Strain when pouring.

9.49 Vegetable potato and meat mash

Strengthens spleen and liver, regulates Qi flow, moisturizes, relaxes, builds up Qi.
Cooking time approx. 30 min
Calories p. portion: 127
2 portions

Quantity of ingredients
Potato 1/4 lbs - 4oz / 100g. (yes)... earth
Carrot (Early Carrot) 5/8 oz / 200g. (recommended) .... earth
Beef meat (calf) 1/8 lbs - 2oz / 40g. (little)................................. earth
Apricots juice 6 table spoons / 60g. (recommended).................. earth
Rapeseed oil 1 table spoon / 6g. (yes)....................................... earth

Cooking instructions:
Remove the flesh, skin, tendons and grease, wash under cool water and cut into small pieces and boil in a little water. After about 15-20 minutes, remove and puree. Wash the vegetables and potatoes, peel and cut into not too small pieces. Cook gently with a little water over a low heat for 10-20 minutes. Use the blender to chop the vegetables. Mix everything, add butter or oil and fruit juice and puree again.

Alternately use other meats such as chicken, lamb or turkey. Also change vegetables with zucchini, kohlrabi, fennel, pumpkin, parsnips and broccoli.

Also change the fruit juices. This can produce a variety of flavors.

9.50 Vegetable semolina soup

Strengthens spleen and liver, regulates Qi flow, builds up Qi, dries out, passes downwardly, reduces moisture, regulates Qi.
Cooking time approx. 20 min
Calories p. portion: 199
3 portions
Allergens: AEGL

Quantity of ingredients
Basic recipe for a vegetable soup 2 cup / 500g. (yes).........................*
Potato 1 piece / 80g. (yes).. earth
Parsnip 1 piece / 180g. (recommended) .... fire
Carrot 1 piece / 120g. (recommended) .... earth
Celery root 3/8 lbs - 6oz / 150g. (recommended) .... earth
Kohlrabi 1/2 piece / 200g. (yes)... earth
Beans (green, fresh) 1/4 lbs / 100g. (yes)................................... water
Wheat semolina 2 table spoons / 24g. (yes) .... wood
Lovage 1/2 teaspoon / 2g. (little).. metal
Butter organic 1 table spoon / 20g. (yes) .... earth
Soy sauce 1 teaspoon / 3g. (little)... water

Cooking instructions:
Worm the prepared vegetable soup; cook the vegetables in the soup softly. Spread some wheatgrass and let it swell. At the end, add lovage-green and a little butter and taste with soy sauce.

10 Effects of food

10.1 Use ingredients: recommendable

Amaranth
Apricots
Apricots juice
Asparagus (green or white)
Barley
Barley malt
Barley not peeled
Blackberry's
Blueberry
Blueberry juice
Bocksdorn fruits (Fructus Lycii, Goji, goji berry dried
Brussels sprouts
Buckwheat
Buckwheat (roasted) Kasha
Buckwheat whole grain
Carp
Carrot
Carrot (Early Carrot)
Carrot juice without sugar
Celery root
Chard
Cherry
Cherry juice
Chicken egg
Chicken meat
Chinese pearl barley
Chrysanthemum blossom tea
Cocoa
Curcuma
Deer meat
Duck (heart)
Duck (slaughtered)
Fish pieces mixed (fresh water)
Flower pollen
Fruit tea
Grape juice red
Grape juice white
Grapes red
Grass carp
Herbs wild
Juniper berry

Kidney beans (red)
Longane
Lotus seeds
Octopus
Parsley
Parsnip
Peaches
Pearl barley
Perch
Plum
Quinoa
Rabbit meat
Raspberry
Raspberry jam
Red berry (without sugar)
Rice (Gaoliang / Sorghum)
Rice (whole grain)
Rice Basmati
Rice black
Rice flour
Rice long grain rice
Rice red
Rice round grain
Rice sweet Rice variety any
Rice wild (nature rice)
Rose hip tea
Salmon
Sesame paste (Tahini)
Sesame, black
Sesame, white
Spinach
Sugar cane sugar
Sugar fructose - fruit sugar
Sugar glucose - grapes sugar
Sugar Milk Sugar
Sugar molasses
Sunflower seeds
Trout
Turkey breast meat
Walnuts
Wheat
Wheat bulgur

10.2 Use ingredients: yes

Acai powder
Adzuki beans
Agave nectar
Almond

Almond marzipan
Almond milk
Almond puree
Aloe juice

Amaranth Pops
Anchovy / Sardine
Angelica root
Apple (sour)
Apple (sweet)
Apple juice (natural cloudy)
Apple puree
Apricot
Apricot nectar
Arrowroot
Artichoke
Balm
Barley flour
Barley grass powder
Barley grouts
Basic recipe for a beef soup
Basic recipe for a chicken soup
(warming)
Basic recipe for a duck soup
Basic recipe for a fish soup
Basic recipe for a rice soup (Congee)
Basic recipe for a vegetable soup
(nutritious)
Basil
Basil (fresh)
Bay leaf
Beans (green, fresh)
Beef bone marrow
Beef heart
Beef heart (calf)
Beer (Pils)
Beer (Top-fermented German dark
beer)
Berries of the season
Berry juice
Black beans
Black caraway
Black fungus mushroom
Blackberry dried (unripe fruit)
Blackberry leaves
Black-eyed peas
Blueberry dried
Blueberry jam
Boletus mushroom
Bread roll
Breadcrumbs (wheat bread, bread roll)
Broad beans (thick beans)
Broccoli
Butter (half fat)
Butter beans white
Butter organic
Calamari
Cardamom
Carob flour, St. john's bread

Cashews
Cauliflower
Celery sticks
Cereal coffee
Chamomile
Chamomile tea
Champignon
Chanterelle
Cherry (sour)
Cherry compote
Chervil
Chervil dried
Chestnut puree
Chestnuts
Chicken egg white
Chicken heart
Chicken liver
Chicken yolk
Chickpeas
Chickweed
Chicory
Chinese cabbage
Chives
Chlorella (fresh water)
Coconut fat
Coconut flakes
Coconut grated
Coconut meat
Coconut milk
Cod
Codfish
Coix (seeds) YiYi Ren
Compote (fruits of the season)
Coriander
Coriander (fresh)
Corn
Corn (fast polenta)
Corn flour
Corn germ oil
Corn Grease (Polenta)
Corn silk tea
Corn starch
Cottage cheese
Couscous
Cranberries
Cranberry
Cream 10% coffee cream
Cream sour 10%
Crucian
Cumin (Caraway seed)
Currant (black)
Currant (red)
Currant (white)
Currant jam (black)

Currant jam (red)
Currant juice (black)
Daisy
Dates dried
Dates red
Deer meat
Deer's Bones
Ducks egg
Dyer's broom herb
Eel
Eel smoked
Elderberries
Elderberry blossom tee
Endive salad
Fenugreek (Trigonella foenum-graecum)
Feta cheese
Fig
Fig dried
Fish innards
Fish remains
Flounder
French beans
Fresh cheese
Fresh cheese from soya
Fresh cheese with herbs
Gelee Royal
Ginkgo fruit
Ginseng
Ginseng root
Gourd
Grapes white
Grapeseed oil
Ground
Ground caraway
Guava
Halibut (Flatfish)
Hazelnuts
Herbal tea mix
Herbs bitter
Herbs of Provence
Herbs various
Herring
Hibiscus tea
Hijiki
Hokkaido pumpkin
Hop
Iceberg lettuce
Jasmine blossoms tee
Kaki plum
Kalmus
King Solomon's-seal
Kohlrabi
Kombu seaweed (Saccharina japonica)

Kudzu
Kukicha tea
Lamb's lettuce
Lavender blossoms
Leaf salads (bitter)
Lemon peel
Lentils
Lentils black
Lentils red
Lentils yellow
Lettuce
Lima beans
Lime blossom tea
Linseed
Linseed (crushed)
Liver smoothing tea
Lovage seeds
Malt
Maple syrup
Margarine
Margarine (diet)
Marjoram
Mediterranean fish (cod, plaice, haddock, sea eel, mackerel)
Millet
Millet flakes
Miso
Miso black (fermented)
Miso paste (soy bean paste)
Morel (black, dried)
Morel, dried
Mung bean
Mustard
Mustard Dijon
Mustard medium hot
Mustard seeds
Mustard sweet
Nori, purple seaweed, red algae
Oat milk
Okra
Olive oil
Olives
Onion (shallot)
Onion (spring onion)
Onion read
Onion white
Orange blossom
Orange dried peel
Orange grated peel
Oyster mushroom
Oysters
Papaya
Parsley root
Peanut (roasted)

Peanut butter
Peanut oil
Peanuts
Pear
Pear juice
Pearl barley
Peas
Peas, green
Pepper (ground)
Pepper white (ground)
Peppercorns
Peppermint
Peppermint tea
Peppers
Peppers (rose peppers)
Peppers (sweet)
Pine nuts
Pistachios
Pomegranate
Potato
Potato (mealy)
Potato flour
Prickly pear
Psyllium seed
Pumpkin
Pumpkin seed oil
Pumpkin seeds
Quince
Rabbit
Radicchio
Radish (white, green, purple-red)
Radish black
Radish horseradish
Radish leaves
Raisins
Rapeseed oil
Raspberry dried (immature)
Raspberry leaf tea
Red cabbage
Reishi mushroom
Rice (fragrance)
Rice malt
Rice mash
Rice noodles
Rice starch
Rice sticky
Romaine lettuce / lettuce salad
Rosefish
Rucola
Rusk
Rye
Rye flour
Rye wholemeal bread
Safflower (Dyer's thistle / Hong Hua)

Saffron
Sage
Sago (cereals)
Sake
Salsify
Savory
Savoy cabbage / kale
Sesame oil
Shiitake, dried
Shrimp
Shrimps
Soy flour
Soy noodles
Soy Tofu
Soybean milk
Soybean oil
Soybeans
Soybeans, black
Soybeans, blacks, fermented
Soybeans, yellow
Spelled (Dark) bread
Spelled flakes
Spelled grain
Spelled semolina
Spelled wholemeal flour
Sugar substitute (sweetener)
Sunflower oil
Sweet potato
Tangerine
Tarragon (Estragon)
Thyme
Thyme dried
Topinambur
Trout (smoked)
Truffle
Tsampa (roasted barley flour)
Turkey ham
Turnip
Valerian
Vanilla
Vanilla pod
Vanilla powder
Vanilla sugar natural
Vegetable juice
Wakame
Water
Water hot
Wax gourd
Wheat flakes
Wheat flour
Wheat flour whole grain
Wheat germ oil
Wheat semolina
Wheat semolina for children

Wheat/Rye/Gray-black bread with yeast
White beans
White bread (baguette)
White bread (pretzel sticks)
White bread (roll)
White bread (wheat bread)
White breadcrumbs

White dumpling bread (wheat bread cut into chunks)
Wormwood herb
Yam root, yam root tuber
Yew nut
Zucchini

10.3 Use ingredients: little

Acerola fruit nectar or powder
Anise (Common Fennel)
Apricot dried
Apricot jam
Baking powder
Banchatee (green tea)
barberry
Basic recipe for a beef soup (warming)
Batavia
Bean oil
Bearberry leaf
Beef fillet
Beef liver
Beef lungs (calf)
Beef meat
Beef meat (calf)
Beef meatbones
Beef Oxtail pieces
Beef soup meat
Bitter orange peel
Blue mallow tee
Borage
Borage oil
Boxhorn clover seeds
Bread with carob kernel flour
Brown ale
Buckbean
Bulgur (cereals)
Bush beans
Buttermilk
Camembert
Capers in olive oil
Caviar
Chicken stomach
Clarified butter
Clementine
Clementines
Clove
Cola drink (low calorie)
Corn (roasted)
Cow's milk (1.5% fat)
Cow's milk (whole milk 3.5% fat)
Cranberry

Cranberry jam
Cranberry juice
Cream sour 20%
Cream sour 30%
Cream, sweet 30%
Creamer
Crème fraiche cheese
Cucumber (bitter)
Cucumber (spicy cucumber)
Curd cheese 20%
Currants (black)
Currants (red)
Deer's kidneys
Dill
Dulse (seaweed)
Edam cheese
Emmental cheese
Fennel seeds ground
Fish sauce
Fruit mix juice
Galangal
Ginger fresh
Goose fat
Gorgonzola
Gouda cheese
Grapefruit dried peel
Green spelt
Greengage
Horehound leaves
Hyssop
Kefir
Kumquats
Lamb kidneys
Lamb liver
Leek
Linseed oil
Loquate / Japanese medlar
Lovage
Mineral water
Mirabelle plum
Mixed Pickles
Mold cheese
Mozzarella

Mulberry fruit
Mulled Wine Spice
Multi-grain bread (gray bread)
Mussels
Nasturtium (nose-twister or nose-tweaker)
Nectarine
Nettles
Octopus
Olives green
Orange jam
Orange juice
Orange peel
Oregano dried
Oregano fresh
Oyster shell powder
Parmesan
Peaches (canned)
Pepper Cayenne
Pheasant
Pickle
Pinto beans speckled
Plum dried
Pork brain
Pork ham
Pork ham cooked
Pork heart
Pork's intestine
Processed cheese 12%
Prosecco
Pudding powder vanilla
Puff pastry
Pumpernickel (dark bread)
Rose hip
Rosemary
Rum
Salt
Salt (herbal)

Sauerkraut (cutted cabbage fermented)
Sea buckthorn
Seacrab
Sesame oil roasted
Sheep's milk
Sheep's milk yoghurt
Sherry (whine)
Sour cherries
Sour cream 15% fat
Sour milk
Sour milk cheese 20%
Soy sauce
Soy Tofu smoked
Soya Cuisine (soy cream)
Spiny lobsters
Spirit
Strawberries
Sugar brown
Sugar candy white
Thistle oil
Tuna
Turmeric (yellow root)
Turnips
Umeboshi paste
Umeboshi plums (Japanese apricots)
Vinegar (Apple vinegar)
Vinegar (Red wine vinegar)
Vinegar Aceto Balsamico
Vinegar Aceto Balsamico white
Wheat bran
Whey
White wine
Wild boar meat
Wild garlic (garlic spinach)
Wild herbs
Wormwood
Yeast

10.4 Do not use contra-acting foods

Agar agar (kelp)
Aubergine
Avocado
Bamboo shoots
Banana
Banana (cooking banana)
Beef kidney
Beef stomach
Beer (alcohol-free)
Beer (alcohol-reduced)
Bitter Lemon
Bitter liqueur
Black tea

Blackberry jam
Burdock root tea
Campari
Cantaloupe
Carambola (Star fruit)
Chili (pod or ground)
Cinnamon ground
Cinnamon sticks
Coffee
Cola drink
Cooking oil
Crab
Cream (30% fat)

Cress
Crispbread
Cucumber
Curd cheese 40%
Curry
Curry paste red
Dandelion (young plants)
Dandelionroots tea
Fennel
Fennel tea
Fernet Branca (herbal bitter liqueur)
Feta cheese
Garlic
Ginger oil
Ginger powder
Ginseng liqueur
Goose
Goose blood
Goose egg
Goose parts
Grapefruit (Pomelo)
Grapefruit juice
Green tea
Honey
Honey wine (Met)
Kiwi
Ladyfingers
Lamb bones
Lamb meat
Lamb shoulder
Lamb's lettuce
Lemon
Lemon juice
Lime
Lobster
Lye roll
Mango
Mango juice
Martini
Muesli
Mullet
Mung bean sprouting
Mutton
Mutton
Noodles (wheat) with egg
Noodles (wheat, lasagne) with egg
Noodles (wheat, ribbon noodles) with egg
Noodles (wheat, spaghetti) with egg
Noodles (whole grain) with egg
Nutmeg
Oat
Oat flakes (whole grain)

Oat flakes roasted
Oat flour
Oat fusion (baby food)
Oat meal
Orange
Pimento
Pineapple
Pineapple (from a can)
Pineapple juice without sugar
Poppy
Pork Bacon
Pork fat (lard)
Pork ham smoked
Pork kidneys
Pork Lard
Pork liver
Pork lung
Pork marrow bones
Pork meat
Pork stomach
Pork/beef sausage (smoked)
processed cheese 30%
Rabbit (wild)
Rabbit liver
Radish
Red wine
Rhubarb
Shark
Sorrel
Sourdough
Spurdog (spiny dogfish, Schillerlocken)
St. Benedict's thistle, blessed thistle, holy thistle, Strawberry jam
Strawberry Juice
Sugar - icing sugar
Sugar white
Toast bread (whole grain)
Tomato
Tomato dried
Tomato juice
Tomato paste
Tomato puree
Watermelon
Wheat beer
Wheat flatbread/pita bread
Whole grain bread
Wholemeal flour
Yarrow tea
Yoghurt vanilla
Yogi tea
Yogurt (natural, 1.5% fat)
Yogurt (natural, 3.5% fat)

11 Herbs and their effects

11.1 Basil

thermal effect: warm
taste: spicy, bitter
Dries out, leads down. Tonifies Yang and Qi, dissolves mucus-cold, eliminates wind-cold.
It has a beneficial effect on flatulence and nausea, relaxing and soothing. Good to fight emphysema, bronchitis, whooping cough, high blood pressure, headache, mouth odor, warts, hiccup, gout, migraine.

11.2 Mugwort

thermal effect: warm
taste: bitter, spicy
Regulates and nourishes bleeding, warms the inside, eliminates wind-cold, eliminates parasites, eliminates heat, wetness, regulates and moves Qi.
Reduces bleeding, alleviates pain. In the kitchen, mugwort is used as a spice for fat food. Since it contains many bitter substances, it boosts fat burning and promotes digestion.

11.3 Savory

thermal effect: warm
taste: bitter
Tonifies kidney yang, heart qi, stomach and spleen qi and warms the middle, moves the liver qi and blood, releases mucous and cold from the lungs, opens the surface, induces wind-cold.
Stomach-strengthening, soothing and appetizing. Ideal for prevent colds, strengthens the immune system. In case of incontinence or nocturnal wetting (not for children), put the beans in liquor for libido.

11.4 Dill

thermal effect: warm
taste: spicy
Moves qi, triggers stagnation, heads up.
The medicinal and spice herb has an antispasmodic effect and stimulates gastric juice production. Good to fight flatulence. Antispasmodic for gastrointestinal discomfort.

11.5 Coriander

thermal effect: warm
taste: spicy
Driving sweat, reducing wind, draining moisture, tonifying and regulating qi, eliminating wind-cold.
The essential oils are appetizing, digestive, cramping and soothing in stomach and intestinal disorders.

11.6 Herbs various

thermal effect: taste:
Stimulates appetite. Effect different.
Appetizing, lots of trace elements and vitamins.

11.7 Cress

thermal effect: cool
taste: sweet
Moves and tonifies qi and blood, diuretic, cools in internal heat, moisturizes lungs, triggers stagnation, heads upwards.
Diuretic, supports urination. Good to fight dry mouth, inner agitation, sore throat, diabetes, kidney stones, gastrointestinal complaints, lung problems, menstrual cramps or cancer.

11.8 Chives

thermal effect: warm
taste: spicy
Directs upward. Tonifies blood, kidney Yang and Qi. Dissolves moisture. Bactericide, prevents cancer, strengthens gastric juice production, promotes digestion and blood circulation, promotes growth, triggers stagnation.

11.9 Lovage

thermal effect: warm
taste: spicy, bitter
Reduces inner wind and moisture, dissolves stagnation, directs upward, warms Yang, regulates and moves Qi, warms inside, dissolves mucus-cold, eliminates wind-cold.
Stimulates digestion, reduces pain. Extracts of the root are used to flush out urinary tract infections and prevent kidney gravel.

11.10   Lily bulbs

thermal effect: cool
taste: sweet, bitter
Tonifies Yin, soothes Shen / Spirit. Moisturizes the lungs, clears heat and
stops coughing.
Calms nerves, good to fight scaly skin. The onions and the petals are
added to ointments in the Orient, which can heal muscles and tendons.
White lily (astringent).

11.11   Parsley

thermal effect: warm
taste: bitter
Nourishes blood and liver, harmonizes liver and spleen, strengthens
eyesight, preserves juices, contracts. Dissolves moisture and warms
Yang.
Stimulates liver function, detoxifies. Forces urinating. Relieves flatulence.
Digestive and menstrual stimulating, birth-accelerating, memory-
enhancing, blood-purifying, skin-smoothing.

11.12   Peppermint

thermal effect: cool
taste: spicy, bitter
Cools heat, expels mucus, dissipates wind-cold and wind-heat, moves
stomach qi, releases congestion, tonifies, regulates and moves qi.
Relaxes, frees the lungs and the nose (inhale), regulates the cycle.
Stimulates bile flow and bile production, antispasmodic in gastrointestinal
disorders, antimicrobial and antiviral.

11.13   Rosemary

thermal effect: warm
taste: bitter
Dries out, leads down. Strengthens the heart, lungs and spleen qi,
strengthens liver blood. Strengthens heart-Yin. Expels spleen heat / cold
moisture. Strengthens spleen and kidney yang.
Promotes digestion, relieves bloating, strengthens lung, spleen and
kidney. Affects the circulation and nerves. Appetizing. Baths help to fight
circulatory disorders as well as with gout and rheumatism.

11.14   Sage

thermal effect: neutral
taste: bitter, spicy
Expels slime, guides down, strengthens Qi, eliminates Wind-Heat,
eliminate heat induced by Yin deficiency.
Good to fight yeast infections. The leaves have a digestive effect and are
used in greasy foods. Antiperspirant effect. Helps to relieve coughing
attacks. Dries out.

11.15   Black caraway

thermal effect: warm
taste: spicy, sweet
Dissolve / transform moisture, tonifyes Yang and Qi, moves blood,
suppresses inner wind.
Detoxifying, immunoregulatory. In addition, the oil should stimulate the
formation of bone marrow cells and generally protect body cells from
viruses.

11.16   Thyme dried

thermal effect: warm
taste: bitter
Strengthens the lungs and spleen. Clears wind-cold, dissolves slime-cold,
tones qi, soothes Shen / Spirit.
Disinfecting. It stimulates the blood circulation, increases the appetite and
helps to digest fat meat better. Strengthens lungs and spleen.

11.17   King Solomon's-seal

thermal effect: neutral
taste: sweet, bitter
Tonifies Yin and Qi, astringent, tonifies blood, eliminates wind-cold / heat-
wetness.
Used to repair wounds or damaged tissue. Good to fight dry cough,
earlier also tuberculosis and dysentery, as well as diarrhea and
hemorrhoids.

11.18 Yam root, yam root tuber

thermal effect: neutral
taste: sweet
Tonifies Yin, Yang and Qi, reduces inner wind, dissolves wetness, warms Yang.
Solves cramps (in the gastrointestinal tract). Digestive through increased bile production. Anti-inflammatory in rheumatic diseases.
Mucolytic agent for coughing. Relief of menopausal symptoms.

11.19 Lemon Balm (fresh)

thermal effect: cool
taste: sour
Soothes Shen / Spirit, regulates and moves Qi, eliminates heat caused by Yin deficiency, tones Qi.
Stimulating, antibacterial, encouraging, relaxing, antispasmodic, cooling, antipyretic, analgesic, sweat-inducing, virus-inhibiting. Good for colds, fever, flu, cough, bronchitis, asthma, loss of appetite, bloating, heartburn.

12 Basics of Nutrition

The basic principles of nutrition described herein are general recommendations. They are not aimed at a specific form of therapy. Recommendations concerning a therapy have priority.

12.1 Nutrition

Regular meals in a relaxed atmosphere. A warm breakfast is considered a good start into the day.
The main meals ought to be taken for lunch – supper in the early evening. Pay attention to feeling hungry or sated: don't eat too much nor remain hungry is the rule
Prepare the meals freshly from natural, regional products. Frozen, heat-conserved, industrially prepared or foodstuffs cooked in the microwave oven are rejected.
Choice of foodstuffs according to the season: more cooling food in summer, more warming food in winter.
Eat cooked food at least twice a day. Food and drinks ought to be lukewarm, never ice-cold or hot.
Raw vegetables, briefly cooked vegetables, freshly squeezed juices and mineral water are not recommended. Milk and dairy products are only included in the diet if they don't cause problems. Don't use therapeutic recipes over a longer period without consulting your doctor or therapist.

Varied food
Enjoy the diversity of foodstuffs. Characteristics of a balanced nutrition are variety, suitable combination and a balanced quantity of rich and low energy foodstuffs (on one hand avoiding undersupply with essential nutrients and on the other hand to take to many undesirable substances).

A lot of Cereal Products - and Potatoes
Bread, pasta, rice, cereal flakes (best wholemeal) as well as potatoes contain almost no fat, but many vitamins, mineral nutrients, trace elements, roughage and secondary plant substances. These foodstuffs ought to be taken with low-fat side dishes.

Vegetables and Fruit – „Take Five" every day … 5 portions of vegetables and fruit a day, as fresh as possible, briefly cooked, or maybe one portion as a juice – ideal as a side dish to every meal as well as snack between meals: Thus a lot of vitamins, mineral nutrients as well as roughage and secondary plant substances

Daily milk and dairy products

Milk and Dairy Products every Day, once or twice per Week Fish; meat, sausages as well as eggs moderately. These foodstuffs contain valuable nutrients like calcium in the milk, iodine selenium and omega-3 fat acids in saltwater fish. Meat is favorable due to its high content of disposable iron and the vitamins B1, B6 and B12. Quantities of 300 – 600 g meat and sausage per week are sufficient. Prefer low-fat products, especially in meat- and dairy products.

Low-fat and fatty Foodstuffs

Fat supplies us with essential fat acids and fatty foodstuffs contain also fat-soluble vitamins. Fat is high in energy; therefore much fat in the food may cause overweight, possibly also cancer. Too many saturated fat acids may further a tendency for cardio-vascular diseases in the long term. Prefer vegetable oils and fats (e.g. rapeseed-, olive-, soya-oils and solid fats produced therefrom). Beware of invisible fat in meat- and dairy products, pastry and sweets as well as in fast-food and convenience foods. 70 – 90 g fat per day is sufficient.

Moderately Sugar and Salt

Take sugar and foods/drinks containing various kinds of sugar (e.g. glucose syrup) only occasionally. Use herbs and spices as well as a little salt creatively. Prefer salt containing iodine.

Plenty of Liquids

Water is absolutely essential. Drink 1-2 l liquids every day. Prefer water (with or without gas) and other low-calorie drinks. Alcoholic drinks should not be taken.

Tasty Dishes, carefully cooked

Cook the meals with as low temperatures and as short as possible, using little water and fat – this preserves the original taste, keeps the nutrients intact and prevents the production of harmful compounds.

Take time and enjoy the food

Take your Time and enjoy your Food
Eating consciously helps to eat right. The eye enjoys food, too. It's fun, invites to enjoy varied dishes and stimulates the feeling of satiety.

Watch your Weight and stay in Motion

A balanced diet and a lot of exercise and sport (30 – 60 min/day) are a healthy combination. The right weight furthers well-being and health.
Thermals, directional effectiveness, digestive power
There are various criteria for judging the effectiveness of herbs and

foodstuffs.

The use of certain herbs and ingredients is based on observations of the effects on the body which these foodstuffs, herbs and spices show after having eaten them. The medical science has developed following system: Every ingredient or herb has a directional effectiveness. Furthermore, there are herbs which have a special effect on certain organs.

The basic condition for a healthy metabolism is to obtain sufficient energy from food and that the digestive process doesn't use too much energy. An easily digestible meal makes content and sated, doesn't cause flatulence and fatigue after the meal. The perfect spices increase the healthiness of our meals. Very often, just small doses of herbs and spices will suffice. They are not used to make us sated, but to help our digestive organs to digest the food.

12.2 Recipes

The recipes list the ingredients to be used and the cooking instructions show how the dish is prepared. The list of ingredients shows the concerned quantities as well as the relevance for the therapy. If you find „less than mentioned", try to comply or find an alternative from the „list of recommended foodstuffs". Mostly it shall result just in a small change of taste when you simply avoid this ingredient.

Mild cooking methods: boiling, stewing, poaching, steaming
Strong cooking methods: barbecuing, roasting, frying, smoking
Balanced cooking methods: deep-frying, baking brick
Deep-freezing and warming in the microwave oven should be avoided (denaturalization).

12.3 Foodstuffs

Foodstuffs have an effect on body and soul like medicinal herbs, only a very much milder one. Dietary advice is mainly based on regional foodstuffs. The knowledge about the effects of each foodstuff and the knowledge, when which foodstuff shall be used, is based on the orthodox school of medicine. Use ecologic-organic products, if possible. As everything should be cooked for a long time due to a better digestability and very rarely eaten raw, the food agrees with everyone.

The classification of the foodstuffs according to their effect on the body is the basis in order to achieve a harmonious status of health.

Dietary advisors do not recommend certain foodstuffs for everyone. The individual diet is tailor-made for the individual constitution.

Buy only fresh and ripe fruit and vegetables. You ought to leave unripe fruit and vegetables and such with brown spots and wilted leaves behind in the market. In this case take deep-frozen goods (never ready-to-serve dishes!). Fruit and vegetables are deep-frozen immediately after harvesting and often contain more vitamins and minerals than the goods from the vegetable shelf. Whereas conserved or tinned goods contain very much less biological substances. Also, salt, sugar and others are mostly added to the latter. Never leave the foodstuffs in the water after washing them to avoid that many vital substances get drowned. Clean salads, fruit and vegetables immediately before serving.

Please make sure of the hygienic processing of foodstuffs. Clean your salads, fruit and vegetables carefully. When cooking with meat, prepare all ingredients first and then process the meat products. Clean the worktop and tools very carefully. Wooden surfaces ought to be treated with a mild disinfectant regularly in order to reduce germination. Store fruit and vegetables separately, if possible. Harvested fruit and vegetables are still alive and emit e.g. ethylene gas, which makes other products ripen and age faster. Keep meat and fish in the closed packaging or store them in the fridge in closed containers.

12.4 Herbs

There are some basic rules for storing medicinal herbs. On principle, herbs must be protected from direct sunlight, humidity and heat.

Containers for the storage of herbs may be glasses, ceramic jars and even plastic containers. However, plastic is a rather unsuitable material and should only be a short-term solution. In case of glass containers, use a dark material.

Medicinal herbs cannot be kept for any long period. The shelf life of herbs is limited. However, it can be prolonged with suitable storage. The place should be dark, rather cool and absolutely dry. A wooden medicine cabinet, placed not directly next to a source of heat, would be ideal. Never buy large quantities of herbs so as not to have to throw them away. Label the container with the name of the herb and the date of harvesting or processing.

13 Other dietic-books

The following syndromes of dietetics, TCM or for a therapy supplement for cancer are available.

E001. **Dietetics** Nutrition of the infant - baby food
E002. Nutrition during lactation
E003. Nutrition in old age
E004. Nutrition of children and adolescents
E005. Nutrition of athletes
E006. Light weight
E007. Pregnancy
E008. Full food

Protein and electrolyte - kidneys
E009. (hemodialysis) dialysis treatment
E010. Acute renal failure
E011. Chronic renal insufficiency
E012. Nephrotic syndrome
E013. Kidney stones (nephrolithiasis)

Gastrointestinal tract - pancreas
E014. Acute pancreatitis (inflammation of the pancreas)
E015. Chronic pancreatitis (inflammation of the pancreas)

Gastrointestinal tract - small intestine and large intestine
E016. Acute obstipation (constipation)
E017. Chronic obstipation (constipation)
E018. Colon irritabile
E019. Diverticulitis
E020. Acquired lactose intolerance (lactose malabsorption)
E021. Fructose malabsorption
E022. Glutensensitive enteropathy (celiac disease)
E023. Colectomy
E024. Short Bowel Syndrome

Gastrointestinal tract - liver, gallbladder, bile ducts
E025. Acute and chronic hepatitis (inflammation of the liver)
E026. Cholelithiasis (bile stones)
E027. fatty liver
E028. cirrhosis

Gastrointestinal tract - Stomach and duodenal intestine
E029. Acute gastritis
E030. Chronic gastritis
E031. Stomach bleeding
E032. Ulcus ventriculi and duodenal ulcer
E033. Condition after gastric surgery

Gastrointestinal tract - oral cavity and esophagus

E034. Stomatitis
E035. Esophageal carcinoma (esophageal cancer)
E036. Refluosophagitis (heartburn)

Special diseases
E037. Phenylketonuria (PKU)
E038. Rheumatic joint diseases

E039. **Metabolism** Obesity (overweight)
E040. Diabetes mellitus
E041. Eating disorders (underweight)

Fat metabolism
E042. Hypercholesterolaemia (increased cholesterol level)
E043. Hepatic Encephalopathy

Heart and circulation
E044. Arteriosclerosis (arterial calcification)
E045. Heart insufficiency
E046. Hypertension
E047. Hyperuricaemia and gout

E048. **Changed nutrient requirements** In case of fever
E049. For malignant diseases
E050. After burns
E051. Radiation and chemotherapy

E100. **CANCER** Pancreatic cancer
E101. Bladder cancer
E102. Blood cancer (leukemia)
E103. Breast cancer
E104. Colorectal cancer
E105. Gastric cancer
E106. Kidney cancer
E107. Esophageal cancer

E200. **TCM** Bladder - moisture heat in the bladder Bladder - moisture and cold in the bladder Bladder - emptiness and cold in the bladder
E201. Large intestine - external cold affects the large intestine Large intestine - moisture heat in the large intestine
E202. Large intestine - heat blocks the intestine II acute
E203. Large intestine - dryness of the colon
E204. Large intestine - Yang deficiency (cold)
E205. Heart - Blood insufficiency
E206. Heart - Blood stagnation
E207. Heart - Fire
E208. Heart - Hot mucus clogs the heart pores
E209. Heart - Cold mucus clogs the heart pores
E210. Heart - Qi deficiency
E211. Heart - Yang deficiency
E212. Heart - Yin deficiency
E213. Liver - Ascending Liver Yang
E214. Liver - Blood deficiency
E215. Liver - Blood stagnation

E216. Liver - Moisture heat in liver and gall bladder Liver - Fire
E217. Liver - Gall bladder Qi-Empty Liver - Cold in the liver meridian
E218. Liver - Qi stagnation Liver - Wind Liver - Wind with ascending liver Yang
E219. Liver - Wind with blood anemic
E220. Liver - Wind with extreme heat
E221. Lung - Qi deficiency Lung - Mucus-moisture in the lungs
E222. Lung - Mucus-heat in the lungs
E223. Lung - Mucus-cold in the lungs
E224. Lung - Dryness of the lungs
E225. Lung - Wind-heat attacks the lungs
E226. Lung - Wind-cold affects the lungs
E227. Lung - Yin deficiency
E228. Stomach - Bloodstagnation Stomach - Fire
E229. Stomach - Cold with liquid
E230. Stomach - Nutrition stagnation
E231. Stomach - Qi deficiency
E232. Stomach - Rebellious Qi
E233. Stomach - Yin Emptiness
E234. Spleen - Heat and moisture attack the spleen
E235. Spleen - Coldness and moisture affects the spleen
E236. Spleen - Qi deficiency
E237. Spleen - Qi deficiency + Declining spleen Qi
E238. Spleen - Qi deficiency + spleen does not control the blood
E239. Spleen - Yang deficiency
E240. Kidney - Heart and kidney no longer communicate
E241. Kidney - Jing deficiency
E242. Kidney - Kidneys cannot receive the Qi
E243. Kidney - Qi is not stable
E244. Kidney - Yang deficiency
E245. Kidney - Yin deficiency

For further information visit di-book.com.